Rain Forests

by Nancy Smiler Levinson

illustrated by Diane Dawson Hearn

NEW GUINEA
Count Raggi's bird

SCHOLASTIC INC.
New York   Toronto   London   Auckland   Sydney
Mexico City   New Delhi   Hong Kong   Buenos Aires

For Merrill Joan Gerber,
who continues to inspire
N. S. L.

With thanks to Charlotte Lucas
And best wishes to Nancy Smiler Levinson
D. D. H.

ISBN-13: 978-0-545-11203-1
ISBN-10: 0-545-11203-6

Text copyright © 2008 by Nancy Smiler Levinson.
Illustrations copyright © 2008 by Diane Dawson Hearn.
All rights reserved. Published by Scholastic Inc.,
557 Broadway, New York, NY 10012, by arrangement
with Holiday House, Inc. SCHOLASTIC and
associated logos are trademarks and/or
registered trademarks of Scholastic Inc.

12 11 10 9 8 7 6 5 4 3 2 1   8 9 10 11 12 13/0

Printed in the U.S.A.   .   23

First Scholastic printing, September 2008

The art for this book was created with acrylic
paint on Strathmore paper.

**baby
orangutan**

king cobra

leaf insect

birdwing butterfly

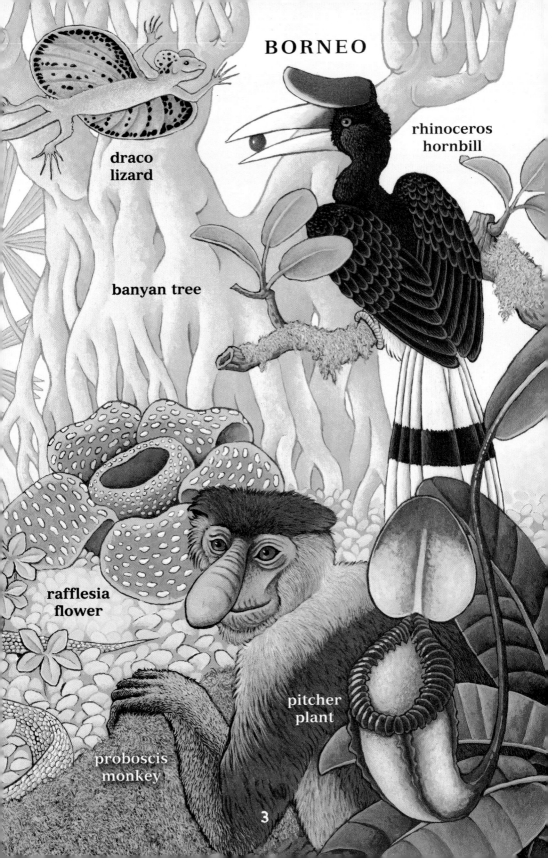

BORNEO

draco lizard

rhinoceros hornbill

banyan tree

rafflesia flower

pitcher plant

proboscis monkey

3

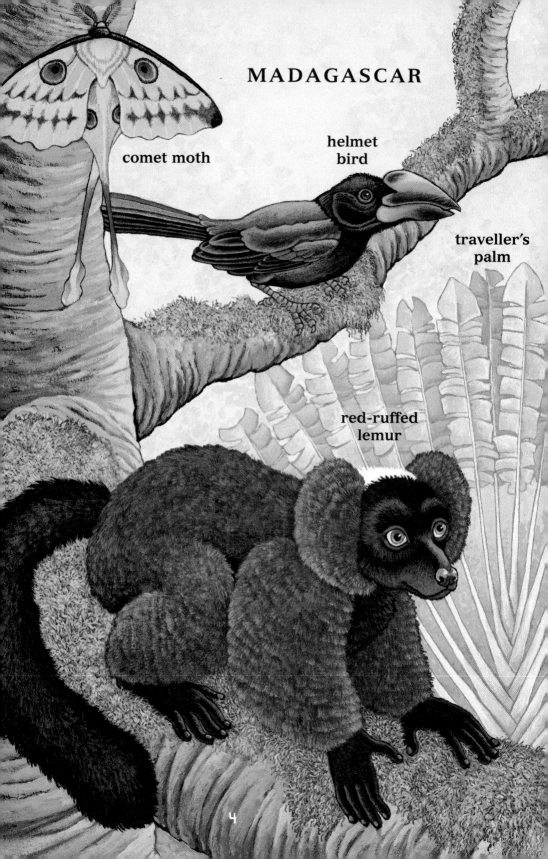

MADAGASCAR

comet moth

helmet
bird

traveller's
palm

red-ruffed
lemur

A rain forest is a wet forest.
It is thick with many kinds of trees
and plants.
Many animals live in it.
Rain falls
most of the year.

silky
sifaka

giraffe-necked
weevil

Parson's
chameleon

Most rain forests grow in hot places near the equator.
They are tropical rain forests.

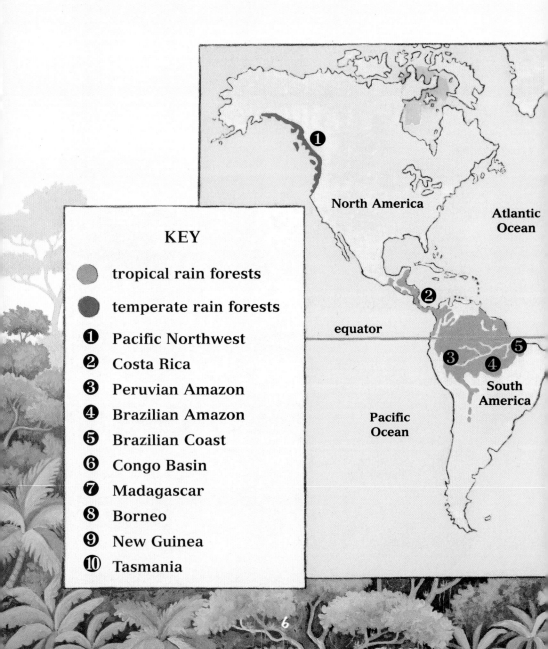

KEY

tropical rain forests

temperate rain forests

❶ Pacific Northwest
❷ Costa Rica
❸ Peruvian Amazon
❹ Brazilian Amazon
❺ Brazilian Coast
❻ Congo Basin
❼ Madagascar
❽ Borneo
❾ New Guinea
❿ Tasmania

North America

Atlantic Ocean

equator

Pacific Ocean

South America

Some grow in cool places.

They are temperate rain forests.

CONGO BASIN

jade-headed beetle

okapi

mahogany tree

lowland gorilla

bamboo

TROPICAL RAIN FORESTS

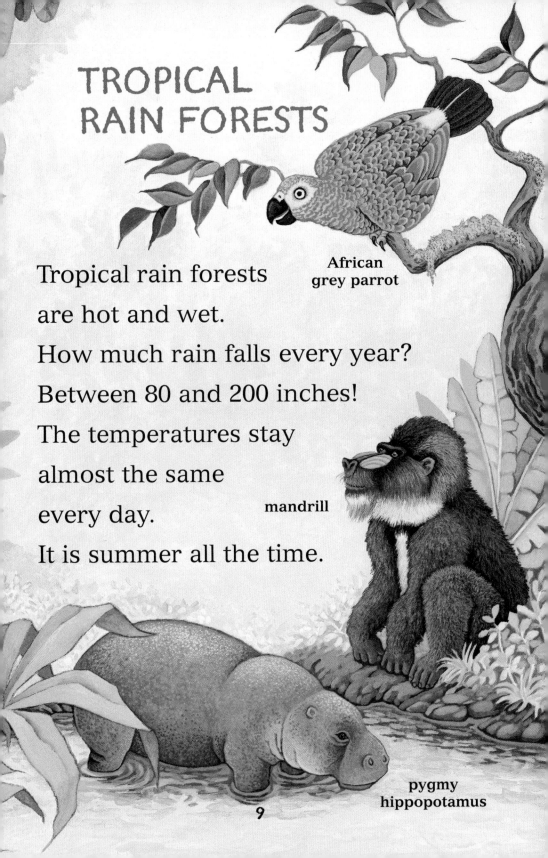

African grey parrot

Tropical rain forests
are hot and wet.
How much rain falls every year?
Between 80 and 200 inches!
The temperatures stay
almost the same
every day.
It is summer all the time.

mandrill

pygmy
hippopotamus

white-throated toucan

palm fruit

ocelot

treehopper

mimosa butterfly

Tropical rain forests are jungles.
They are filled with trees, plants,
and vines.
Thousands of kinds
of animals live in them.

Peruvian dung beetle

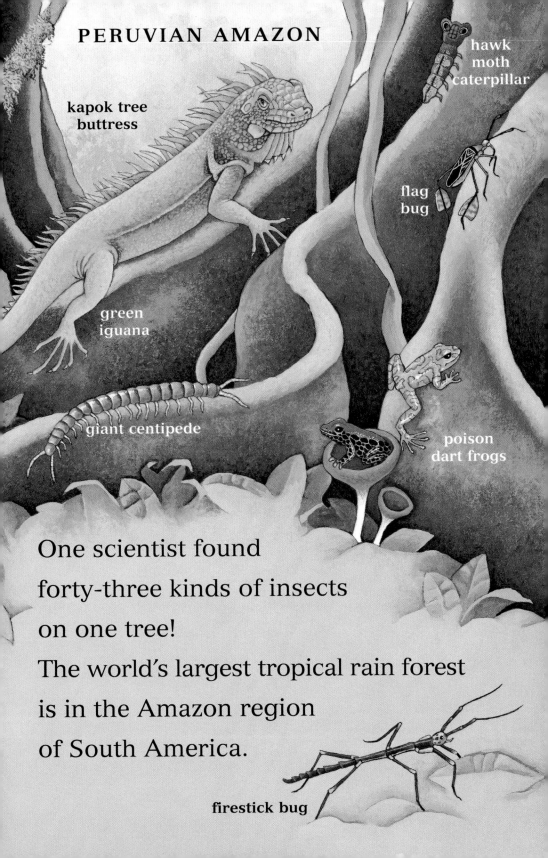

hawk moth caterpillar

kapok tree buttress

flag bug

green iguana

giant centipede

poison dart frogs

One scientist found
forty-three kinds of insects
on one tree!
The world's largest tropical rain forest
is in the Amazon region
of South America.

firestick bug

Rain forests have four layers.
Each layer has its own life-forms.
The top layer is called *emergent*.
The emergent trees poke above
the rest of the forest into the sunlight.
Eagles and parrots live there.

red howler
monkeys

kapok
treetop

BRAZILIAN AMAZON

harpy eagles

ipe tree

blue-headed parrots

13

The second layer is a closed *canopy*.
It is a living roof
that covers the forest below.
It is formed by treetops
that grow close together.

banana
tree

green-headed
tanager

gladiator
tree frog

spider
monkeys

scarlet
macaws

tayra

15

wasp

pygmy marmoset

yolk
butterfly

squirrel
monkey

monkey
ladder
vine

16

Monkeys eat berries and fruits.
Butterflies and hummingbirds
drink nectar from flowers.
Big stinging wasps
crawl across leaves.
This is the most lively layer of all.

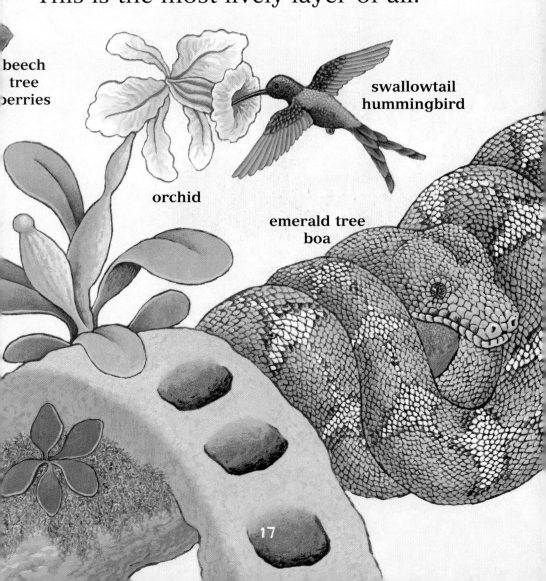

beech
tree
berries

orchid

swallowtail
hummingbird

emerald tree
boa

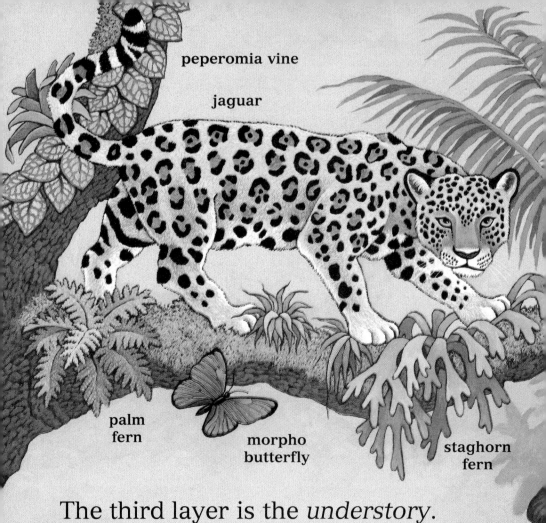

peperomia vine

jaguar

palm
fern

morpho
butterfly

staghorn
fern

The third layer is the *understory*.

It gets little sunlight.

Sun cannot get through the canopy.

Few flowers grow.

Jaguars wait in trees

to leap down

and catch prey on the ground.

cannonball
tree

coatimundi

mamey
tree

bare-faced
curassow

collared
puffbird

passion
flower
vine

vine
snake

moonflower

coendou

pigmy
owl

strangler
fig

anteater
(tamandua)

honeybear
(kinkajou)

Bats fly at night to feed.
Some catch three thousand insects
in one night's flight.

round-eared bats

sorcerer
moth

night monkey

vampire bat

The fourth layer is the *forest floor*.
It is dark and eerie.
It is filled with
plants, mosses, ferns, dead leaves,
and billions of ants.

ground
fern

capybara

caiman

apple snail

Victoria
amazonia
water lily

piranha

hoatzin
and baby

walking tree

green
anaconda

moss

leafcutter ants

Hercules beetle

23

brocket
deer

heliconia

saddleback
caterpillar

pink-toed
tarantula

stink
beetle

Army ants march in swarms
and eat everything in their paths.
Termites live in colonies and eat wood.
Deer and wild pigs are hard to see,
but insects can be seen everywhere!

three-toed
sloth

Many animals live in the trees
most of their lives.
Some tree frogs never touch the ground.
They have sticky toe pads
to help them climb slippery leaves.
Sloths hang upside down all the time—
even when they eat and sleep.

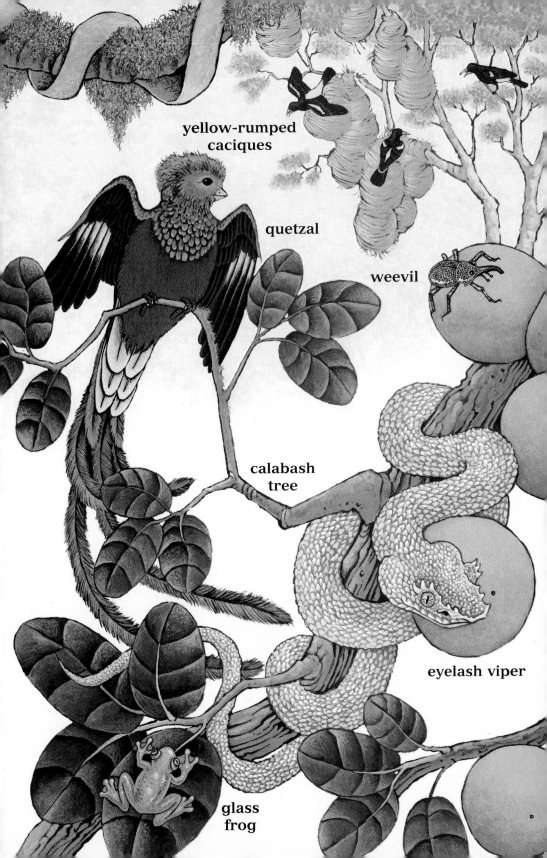

yellow-rumped
caciques

quetzal

weevil

calabash
tree

eyelash viper

glass
frog

Most plants need roots in soil
to get water and food.
Air plants do not.
They grow on tree trunks and
get water and food from the air.
They are called *epiphytes*.
Orchids and bromeliads
are epiphytes.

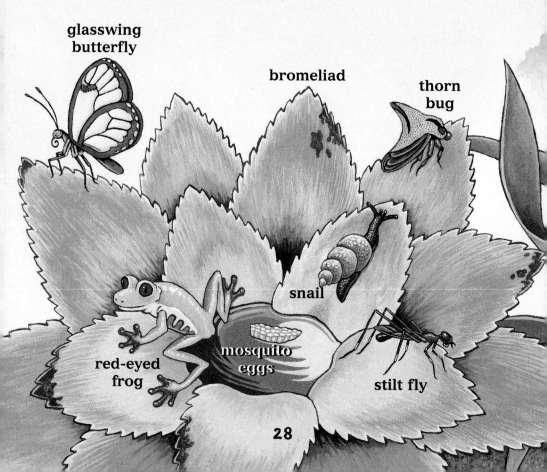

glasswing
butterfly

bromeliad

thorn
bug

snail

red-eyed
frog

mosquito
eggs

stilt fly

28

COSTA RICA

orchid

fiery-throated
hummingbird

bromeliad

scarab
beetle

orchid

bromeliad

capuchin
monkey

northern
spotted
owl

Sitka
spruce

bald eagle

licorice
fern

mule
deer

PACIFIC
NORTHWEST

cougar

black bear cub